A first-time author who started writing after the loss of a much-loved dog which coincided with the Covid-19 Pandemic and first lockdown.

After 33 years in Education — teaching, advising, and inspecting in Secondary schools in London communities Pam retired. Since then she spends her time reading, gardening, walking and travelling extensively. She enjoys Ballet, Cinema, Opera, Theatre and living for part of the year in Perth, Western Australia.

THE DOG Who ARRIVED In A BOX

A Short Story About A Very Special Dog

PAMELA BELMOUR

AUSTIN MACAULEY PUBLISHERS™

LONDON • CAMBRIDGE • NEW YORK • SHARJAH

A CIP catalogue record for this title is available from the British Library.

ISBN 9781398444072 (Paperback)
ISBN 9781398444089 (Hardback)
ISBN 9781398444096 (ePub e-book)

www.austinmacauley.com

First Published 2022
Austin Macauley Publishers Ltd®
1 Canada Square
Canary Wharf
London
E14 5AA

To: Den, Sveta, Lala and everyone whose pet was not with them during the Covid-19 Pandemic and lockdowns.

Den for his support, good humour and patience.

Seiji and Sveta for moving next door with Kai and always sharing him.

Sveta for her generosity, courage and fortitude.

Lala for long-distance encouragement and technical support.

Austin Macauley Team throughout the process and believing in the book.

One day, a box was delivered to a beautiful house in France. Inside the box was a beagle puppy with a shiny black coat, long ears and slightly crossed brown eyes. The puppy was named Kai which means sea in Japanese. Kai lived with a Japanese man and his wife.

As a puppy, Kai was very playful. He would chew slippers, steal socks and shoes and run away with them. One day, Kai fell into the swimming pool and from that day on, he did not like water—except to drink. Kai was taken to Obedience Training School. Although his owners tried very hard, Kai had a mind of his own and could be very stubborn.

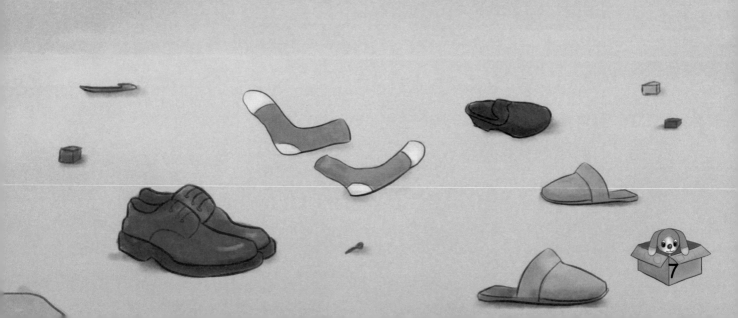

Kai's friend in France was a golden retriever called Shiloh. Kai loved Shiloh and Shiloh loved Kai. Kai showed him all his toys and they played together. Shiloh and Kai were taken for a walk in the forest. Kai ran away because he loved running. He could run very fast. Shiloh's owner was very worried. She knew how much Kai's owners loved him. Everyone looked for him. Many hours later, Kai was found sitting in the spot where the car had been parked. He was a very mischievous dog.

After some time, Kai's owners moved to England. Kai travelled with them in a special crate in the aeroplane. The pilot made sure that Kai was comfortable by turning up the heating. He told all the passengers that Kai was on board. From the airport Kai went to a new house.

There were twelve new houses and two old houses on the street where Kai lived.

Kai knew everybody and everybody knew him. He was given his own room in the new house because he was a very special dog.

In his room was his bed and lots of toys; a leopard cat, a soft bone with his name on it, a hamburger, many balls, a kangaroo and his favourite toy—an elephant. He played with the elephant every day.

Kai loved going for walks
and on those walks, he loved
chasing squirrels, cats
and foxes.

On one walk, a big ginger
cat chased him. He was
very surprised.

He especially loved treats. His favourite treat was a small piece of cheese every night at bedtime.

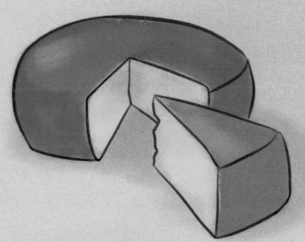

Kai also loved head massages, chasing balls and opening his Christmas and birthday presents. Every Easter, he was given a chocolate egg. This was made with special chocolate just for dogs. One Easter, he buried the egg in his owners' bed.

He also liked hiding in the bushes above the railway sleepers in the garden. He spent a lot of time patiently looking out of the kitchen window, watching the children play in the street or waiting for his owner to come home.

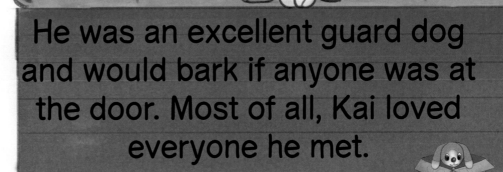

He was an excellent guard dog and would bark if anyone was at the door. Most of all, Kai loved everyone he met.

He did not like rain, loud noises
from cars or lawn mowers, going
to the vet and fireworks.

Like most beagles, Kai was always hungry. On one occasion, he ate nine cupcakes; fortunately, he did not get sick.

He used to sit underneath the table waiting for bits of food.

He enjoyed rides in the car and went on a bus and train too.
Sometimes, when his owner got ready to do some exercises or yoga, Kai would try to join in by lying on the mat. He liked to be very close to people. He rolled on the grass after having a shower, slept in the sun and when it was very hot, he would enjoy treats hidden in ice-cubes placed inside a water bottle.

One day, soon after his ninth birthday, Kai became very sick. He went to see the vet who gave him some medicine but after sixteen days, Kai did not get any better and when he went to see the vet again, he did not return home.